# Lighthearted Intercourse

### A Play

## Bill Naughton

### Samuel French
www.samuelfrench-london.co.uk
www.samuelfrench.com (US)

# LIGHTHEARTED INTERCOURSE

This version of *Lighthearted Intercourse* was adapted by David Thacker from ten drafts of the play and Bill Naughton's handwritten notes. It was first performed at the Octagon Theatre, Bolton, on 4ᵗʰ October, 2012 with the following cast:

| | |
|---|---|
| **Joe** | Nicholas Shaw |
| **Madge** | Fiona Hampton |
| **Visitor** | David Fleeshman |
| **Clara** (Recorded voice) | Maxine Peake |
| **Albert** (Recorded voice) | Peter Kay |
| | |
| **Director** | David Thacker |
| **Designer** | Janet Bird |
| **Lighting Designer** | Mick Hughes |
| **Movement Director** | Lesley Hutchison |
| **Sound Designer** | Andy Smith |
| **Casting Directors** | Beverley Keogh and David Martin |
| **Assistant Director** (Placement) | Hannah Drake |
| **DSM** (On the book) | Sophia Horrocks |

# CHARACTERS

**Joe**, an out-of-work music shop salesman
**Madge**, Joe's wife
**Visitor**
**Clara**, a knocker-up
**Albert**, a neighbour

The play is set in a small house in an industrial street in Bolton

Time — November, late 1920s

ACT I: the bedroom

SCENE 1   Early morning

SCENE 2   A few minutes later

ACT II: the kitchen

SCENE 1   A few minutes later

SCENE 2   Evening of the same day

SCENE 3   A year or so later

## COPYRIGHT MUSIC

# ACT I

## Scene 1

*Late 1920s dance band music such as "Me and My Shadow", "I Can't Give You Anything But Love, Baby", "The Song is Ended", etc. It is lively but with a melancholy overtone*

*House Lights fade. Lights up. Hold the music as long as it will stand up*

*A bedroom of a small house in a working-class street in Bolton. It is early on a cold, dark, November morning, and the scene is lit in a dreamy, unreal glow. Outside it is foggy and wet. The room is bare and poverty stricken, but in no way squalid, and in its simplicity looks almost cosy. We see an old-fashioned brass bedstead on which hang a pair of socks and a pair of trousers. An old army topcoat is on top of the bed as an extra blanket. Near the bed is a baby cot made from a papered over orange box. Beside the bed there is a rickety chair. On the chair is an enamel wash bowl inside of which is a cheap tin alarm clock lying on its side. There is a loud, strong ticking*

*Joe and Madge, a young married couple, are asleep in bed. Madge has got the bedclothes over her side of the bed. Joe turns over, pulling the clothes with him, and Madge turns over almost with him and snuggles up close to him. We hear the usual cosy sleeping sighs and sounds. We hold the scene for a time. The alarm clock is ticking*

*Suddenly the peace is shattered by the sound of a sharp, loud tattoo of wires, struck against a nearby window. The strange sound is heard again. It is from the wire whisk of Clara, the knocker-up*

**Clara** (*off*) Albert! Albert! Can you hear me, Albert! Wake up now! It's five and twenty minutes past five. An' a topcoat colder than yesterday. Come on — up with you! No hanging about!

*We hear a further tattoo. Joe wakes*

Albert! I know you've heard me and you're not letting on!
**Joe** Who wouldn't hear a voice like that!

**Clara** (*off*) But you won't get away with it. I'll be back — and I'll get you, buggerlugs!

*Joe gets out of bed in his short shirt*

**Joe** (*to the audience*) You wouldn't think it was human would you? That's old Clara, the knocker-up.

**Clara** (*off*) Albert! Come on now. Up with you. Have you gone bloody dead! Get up! Get up, you lazy sod!

**Joe** She's not calling me. She's calling the chap next door. Albert Shuttleworth. He's a muckmiser down at the Corporation sewage yard. No short time on that job! She earns her fourpence a week from him! (*He realizes he is without trousers. He goes to the bedrail and talks as he puts on his trousers*) Excuse me — I'd better get my keks on. You'd never think to look at me that a twelvemonth back I was the most eligible bachelor in Bolton, would you? I'm not coddin'. Or shall we say, one of 'em. This is what marriage does to you. Bloody shame, isn't it? I could cry for myself. In fact I do most nights. And I used to be such a lighthearted lad.

*The tattoo is heard again on a nearby window*

**Clara** (*off*) Albert! I'm warning you, you better not be late for your work.

**Joe** He won't — don't you worry! There's too many waiting for his job. And I'm one of them. One of Britain's three million unemployed. Two million, eight hundred and fifty-three thousand, to be more exact.

**Clara** (*off*) Albert – it's turned half-past!

**Joe** That was a short five minutes, Clara! Hey, don't let on but I love it. I mean being at home all day with Madge and our little Lionel. Except folk talk. Her mother for one.

**Clara** (*off; departing*) I know you've heard me. I'll be back. I'll catch you when I've been to the top of the street. And I won't call you again. I'll come in and drag you out of flamin' bed.

**Joe** What a neighbourhood! I come from Great Lever. Quite posh up there. Well, I've always looked on myself as that bit better class — you might have noticed it, I mean the way I speak and that. Just that bit refined. I've never worked in the mill. I used to work at Ackroyd's, the violin and music shop — been there since I left school — Mr Ackroyd's favourite pupil I was, on the piano — I could fiddle a bit too — and I had the best voice in the church choir. I had a full week's holiday a year, with pay, and two pounds one-and-sixpence a week wages. Talk about a bobby's job! It was practically unheard of! (*He*

*places his fingertips on his scalp and firmly presses and rotates*) Oh,
excuse me, I musn't forget my scalp massage. I've a feeling I've been
losing my hair. It seems you begin to lose every bloody thing once
you get wed. It's a fact though, isn't it? Ee, but I used to have some
grand sideboards — down to here they were. They called me Rudy
— y'know, after Valentino. I had to get rid of 'em when I went on
the dole — my sideboards I mean. The way that clerk used to look at
me across the counter — as though I were getting money under false
pretences. Then Madge's mother said it didn't look nice being out of
work and going around looking like a flaming Spaniard. Especially as
I'd soon be claiming an extra two-bob a week for the child that was
on the way. And her dad kept going on about how they could stop my
dole if the supervisor happened to be one way out. It's funny how
old people have this thing against youth. They can't bear you not to
knuckle under and be just like them. Of course they don't like anyone
to be different — not around these parts. I was beginning to feel they
might be right, so one Saturday night, when I was feeling depressed,
I just shaved them off. Madge cried her eyes out when she first saw
me. I came out of the back kitchen like and she stared at me — then
she burst into tears. They're trying to make you look ordinary, Joe, she
said. Me — ordinary I said! They'll have a job on, they will an' all! Do
you know it nearly set me off crying. It goes to show how vulnerable
a young man is. But I'll tell you what — the real joy of my life was
dancing — oh, dancing — I went dancing six nights a week. I used to
look forward to it all day long. Well, I mean I was the kingpin at the
Palais — or one of 'em — the dames were after me like flies round a
jampot. I'd have a different partner for almost every dance. I couldn't
bear sitting a dance out. It was rare I could get more than a yard or
two in the Ladies' Choice — they were practically fighting over me —
they came at me from all sides — one'd have one arm and one t'other.
And I used to love having my pick of the dames for the slow foxtrot.

*The Lights slowly change to give a dance hall effect. We hear the music
of "Miss Annabelle Lee."*

*Joe starts doing a few solo foxtrot steps. He straightens his imaginary
tie, combs his hair, pats down the bottom of his imaginary jacket, and
smoothes it over his behind, then gives the crease of his trousers a hitch
over an imaginary shoe, all in time with the music. Madge gets out of
bed, wearing an old shirt of Joe's. She comes up to Joe without looking
at him. Joe's gaze follows her. Madge gives a half turn and Joe gives her
the eye. They begin to dance, never allowing their eyes to meet. Joe, very
much in charge, hints at considerable skill and style but it is all done*

*with an economy of movement and he allows Madge to do all the work.*
*It looks rather like master and slave with both enjoying the act. Joe talks*
*to the audience through the dance*

I'd three suits that had never seen the inside of a pawnshop. A Saturday
night suit for dancing in — that was a black jacket and striped trousers
— I used to wear that on the monkey run on Bradshawgate — posh
side. Then I'd a Sunday suit — my blue serge, twenty-two ounce
Botany wool, double breasted waistcoat, barrelled jacket — but why
go on — I was one of the best dressed men in Bolton. I'd always line
up some dame or other for the last waltz and take her home. I loved a
nice spoon and cuddle up against a petty in the back street — and that
lovely warm feeling they've got after they've been dancing all night.
But I was always careful not to give them any ideas, see. Fat lot of use
it turned out in the long run.

*The dance comes to an end*

(*To Madge*) Go and grab your things before the last waltz — and I'll
see you outside.

*Madge puts on the old army topcoat and picks up a handbag*

*The Lights change to a backstreet gloom*

**Madge** (*in a broad accent*) Don't forget, I've got to be in by eleven.
**Joe** So have I. If I'm lucky.
**Madge** You picked a right draughty back gate. I feel starved with the
cold.
**Joe** Don't worry — I'll soon warm you up.
**Madge** Has anybody ever told you you've got lovely eyelashes, Joe?
**Joe** Aye. My mother. Here, gimme your bag will you?
**Madge** What for?
**Joe** What d'you think — so's you can put your arms round me.
**Madge** Don't you be so cheeky.

*Madge gives Joe a friendly, but quite hefty thump. Joe takes her bag. He*
*brushes down the back of his imaginary jacket with one hand*

**Joe** Here — wouldn't you be more comfortable like, resting against
the wall?
**Madge** Aye — and get my coat all mucky! You're not daft are you?
How's your mother for soap!

**Joe** Up to the neck in lather.

*They partly embrace, surveying each other. Then Joe turns Madge a little, nuzzles his face up against her and kisses her throat*

**Madge** Ooh, you're a right sloppy thing.
**Joe** (*to the audience*) Oh aren't women lovely. It almost makes you wish you were one. Hey, what am I saying!

*Joe kisses Madge*

**Madge** Hey — you're not a bad spooner, if you are a bit sloppy. Now don't start giving me any of those funny kisses.
**Joe** What funny kisses?
**Madge** You know! What they say the French do.
**Joe** Why — do you fancy one?
**Madge** Get off! I'd as soon chew a penn'orth of tripe bits!
**Joe** Take a deep breath — I'm going to kiss you again.
**Madge** Oh, you're a passionate devil, Joe Eckersley!

*They kiss passionately*

**Joe** Mind if I unfasten your coat?
**Madge** I've not just come over on an onion boat, yu'know!
**Joe** I was only asking.
**Madge** You've got a bad name, Joe Eckersley, for giving girls a rough time!
**Joe** Have I!
**Madge** Well, see you behave yourself.
**Joe** I always do...

*Joe unfastens Madge's coat*

Oh, that's lovely and warm — except when I forget...
**Madge** Well, see as you don't forget tonight.
**Joe** (*to the audience*) She's softening up a bit. I thought she might. I've a feeling it's going to be worth the tuppence tramfare!
**Madge** Now don't you start letting your hands stray.
**Joe** I'm not letting anything stray.
**Madge** Well, just see as you don't.
**Joe** But I've no intention.
**Madge** Well. I'm only warning you not to let them stray — I'm not that sort of girl.

**Joe** But——

**Madge** It'll be too late when I give you a clout with my handbag.

**Joe** *(to the audience)* You know, I think that's how they put the idea into a chap's head — keep harping on you've not to do it!

**Madge** Hey — fingers!

**Joe** What!

**Madge** I won't tell you again! I'll clout you one! Besides, you know what happens just about now.

**Joe** What happens just about now!

**Madge** The Sergeant comes round flashing his torch.

*They kiss passionately. A torch flashes. Joe and Madge break from their passionate kiss, breathless*

*The Lights change to a dreamy, unreal glow*

**Clara** *(off)* Albert! Do you realize what time it is! Get up, you idle sod! Or I'll come an drag you out of bloody bed!

**Joe** Bloody hell, I'd forgotten about the knocker up.

**Albert** *(off)* I'm up, I'm up, I'm up, I'm up! Of course I'm bloody up — up an' bloody near dressed — so shut up and bugger off!

*Madge goes back to bed*

**Joe** Bloody hell — I'd forgotten all about yon chap! What a way to talk to a lady.

**Clara** *(off: departing)* Bugger off yourself, you cheeky sod. I got you up, anyway.

**Joe** Aye, go off into the next street, Clara, if you don't mind. *(To the audience)* What some folk have to do to earn fourpence a week! Well, you can see what a marvellous love life I was having. But when you live in these streets, mile after mile of nothing but bricks and mortar, and pavement and cobble stones. You get as if your soul can hardly breathe.

"How dull it is to pause, to make an end,
To rust unburnish'd, not to shine in use!
As tho' to breathe were life."

I love that line "As though to breathe were life". Some folk think it is. I've always been fond of poetry. I'm considered a bit of an intellectual — in Bolton that is. My mam kept me on at school until I was nearly sixteen. Come to think of it, that's a funny thing — how your own mother can lose interest in you once you get wed. I thought she'd give me the piano for sure — after all she can't play it — but not likely. She said it makes a nice piece of furniture. Now if you want to know how it comes about that a chap like me finds himself in this situation, I'll tell you. Somehow I found I was going out with Madge there regular. On top of dancing with her and taking her home — I found myself taking her for the occasional walk — nothing serious — we weren't courting or anything — at least I didn't think so — just on hand under blouse terms. We hadn't been intimate or anything like that. I'm a Catholic see — but it doesn't mean because a chap goes to church he's not fond of a bit of that there. It all started one wet Saturday night in a stone quarry of all places. That first time I kind of went weak at the knees and had spots in front of my eyes. Something around here is terrific, I thought — but what it was I couldn't make out. I thought a boulder or something would drop on my head.

**Madge**  I wish to hell it had.

**Joe**  Now I'm not a chap to abandon myself to lust but once the ice was broken — if I can put it that way...

**Madge**  You can put it any flamin' way you like — so far as I'm concerned. Go on — out with it — if you're confessing. Don't be ashamed.

**Joe**  I found intimacy began to take place regularly — twice a week, Sundays and Wednesdays as a rule. You see on Wednesday they'd only a piano playing instead of the full band and so we'd slip off a bit early. Make up for it see. Somehow it never struck me as a proper mortal sin — dipping my wick beside the canal towpath of a wet Wednesday night. It seemed like God wasn't looking — especially in Bolton! Sunday in the parlour was quite different of course! I mean it's a tremendous moment for a man. Madge there would think nothing of bringing me along twice on the trot. I think she imagined it brought us closer together. I suppose a woman feels she's got power over a man. I don't know why I'm going into all these details but personally I'm finding it all most interesting. I hope you are. Anyway, one night she comes and she tells me she thinks — guess what? Yes you're right! A mate of mine called Gussy Davies used to go dancing and one time I heard him spouting about how it was impossible for a woman to conceive if you did it standing up. "It stands to reason" he said. "Nature never intended you to do it that way. It would have to be very exceptional" he said. Well in my case it turned out to be very exceptional. But isn't it pitiful when you come to think of it — how a young chap goes round thinking he's getting something for nothing — and fancies he's so smart — and the next thing he's hooked.

**Madge**  (*to the audience*) Hooked! What about me? The way he's going on you'd think he had nowt to do with it. They never give a thought to the woman.

**Joe** It was a right nasty shock — except I was just that bit pleased with myself that I could make one — you know what I mean. I'd had no intention of marrying Madge — for one thing I felt I wasn't in love with her — there was another girl in my thoughts see — and for another thing she was just that bit common. When I got round to informing my mother she shook her head and said: "Nay lad, not one of them Birtwhistles from Daubhill — tha has slipped up there — she's from the wrong end of the town."

**Madge** Who's from the wrong end of the town! Eh! I'm warning you — you'd better not cast any more of your aspersions — I've had as good broughtings-up as you any bloody day in the week. My dad were a skilled man — a textile fitter. He's erected machinery all over Europe — and you can't even knock a nail in a flamin' piece of wood.

**Joe** I've said nothing against your father. I'm not a snob or anything but if you come from the Daubhill area you've a job to hide it.

**Madge** You think you're somebody just because you'd oilcloth on your stairs — oh an' your piano, an' your bloody tippler closet — never heard the end of that.

**Joe** I beg your pardon but I've never swanked about our tippler closet.

**Madge** No you only spent the whole of one Saturday teatime explaining how it worked! And there were all that fuss about your mam having kept you on at school an extra five minutes.

**Joe** You've never heard me boast about my education.

**Madge** No you're a silent brag — coming out with your fancy bloody words no one else has ever heard of. Your mam were never done going on about how you were picked to be the bloody Field Marshal to t'Queen at the Catholic Scholars' Walking Day.

**Joe** Earl Marshal.

**Madge** Earl Marshal then. When I went to tea at your house the first thing I saw were the picture of you there on the piano — all togged up in flaming velvet attending on the queen — that Mary thingamabob.

**Joe** Please keep her name out of it. And listen, Madge, I was only seven when that was taken.

**Madge** Yes and you've never flaming got over it! Cath'lic, only child and mamma's boy into the bargain — no wonder you've turned out such a soft sod.

*Madge goes back under the covers. Joe speaks intimately to the audience*

**Joe** Mary Carlisle she was. She was far above me. Cotton waste merchants they were — lots of money — whereas my mam only

scraped up enough for my costume through taking in washing. I was
madly in love with her. At seven. I couldn't eat for thinking of her.
My mam used to give me doses of castor oil and I'd think, "Mam,
if only you knew". Anyway I felt I ought to do the right thing by
Madge — if only for the sake of the child. And the real big slump hit
town. With three quarters of the town on the dole and the other quarter
on three days a week, nobody wanted to know about music. I mean,
most of them were only sent to learn so that they'd have a second
job at their fingertips — picture palace pianists, see — and Ackroyd's
had to shut up shop. Ackroyd didn't go bankrupt — he died, flamin'
heartbroke. I can see myself standing there at the altar with Madge
beside me — I'd been to sign on the dole that very morning and she
must have been three months gone although it didn't show, her being
young, see, and well built — but of course everybody knew, although
they pretended they didn't — and as I stood there, with the priest
joining us in holy matrimony, I said to myself, "Joe, you'll remember
this moment to your dying day — all the glory has passed from your
life for evermore".

*The Visitor enters. He is a man of mature age, dressed in expensive
looking clothes: a dark sober well cut suit with a white shirt and black
tie. He exudes an air of success and well-being. He is obviously a man
of some substance in the best North country fashion, used to giving
orders, and quite pleased with himself*

And as I was putting the ring on Madge's finger, I'll tell you what I
was wishing — I was wishing — if only it were Mary — the girl I
really love...
**Visitor** You'd no bloody right.

*Joe turns and sees the Visitor*

**Joe** Eh — who are you? Did you speak?
**Visitor** Aye I said you'd no bloody right! To stand there at the altar
being joined in matrimony to one woman and wishing it were another.
You get in bed beside one woman and dream of the other. You've got
neither woman properly. I've often wondered what it was that was
wrong with our marriage and I see it now — I reckon you put the
bloody poison in at the start.
**Joe** Do I know you?
**Visitor** No but I know you! Only too bloody well.
**Joe** You've come to the wrong shop. I mean if you're looking for any
help.

*The baby cries. The Visitor goes towards the baby. Joe crosses to the cot*

**Visitor**  There's a lad, Lionel. Bless him! They're at their best at that
  age.
**Joe**  Lovely little boy he is, though I say it as shouldn't, being his
  father.

*The Visitor turns from the cot and examines the room and everything
in it*

**Visitor**  Ee, but I do like this place — it might not have all mod cons but
  by gum it's homely! I never realized it.
**Joe**  Where've you been! Just look what we need. We need some proper
  curtains, something on the floor, a new cot for the child — that's only
  a flamin' orange box papered over.
**Visitor**  It wouldn't make you happy. You're not going to know anything
  better than this. Not in this life. If you'd any sense, you'd make life
  in this room your reality — not all the crap going on in your bloody
  head.
**Joe**  Have you called about something special, or did you just drop in
  like?
**Visitor**  I dropped in.
**Joe**  I thought you were off to a funeral.
**Visitor**  I was driving along on the motorway, you know, when suddenly
  I...
**Joe**  He's escaped — from Winwick Asylum — without a doubt. He
  must have got over the wall. I'll bet they're after him, but he seems
  harmless enough. Funny, but he reminds me of somebody.
**Visitor**  I was going to the airport. Madge said, "Let Gussy drive you".
  But I said, "You'll need him for shopping". He's getting on a bit but
  he's very willing is Gussy — do anything he's told. (*His attention
  strays to Madge*) Ee, isn't she bonny! I never realized how bonny. I
  could fall in love with her all over again! You sleep together do you —
  in the one bed every night in the week?
**Joe**  Eh? Well, what else?
**Visitor**  Ee, it must be lovely.
**Joe**  Well, not really. The bed sags in the middle, you see and sometimes
  your bodies seem to get all tangled up so that you're practically on top
  of one another all the time. Some nights I've a job to know Madge's
  limbs from mine.
**Visitor**  That's when you start dreaming about this — this...
**Joe**  Mary. I genuinely loved her — since I was that high ——
**Visitor**  What do you know about love? Who told you you were put here
  to pick and choose who you love?

**Joe** — we went to school together — shared the same desk — then she went on to Mount St Joseph's Convent school. It broke my heart... I never saw her again for years — until one Easter Sunday morning, at the holy water font near the porch, as we were coming out of Mass — I was dipping my hand in the font, you see, and I saw this hand outstretched, but unable to reach the holy water because of the people crowding by — so on impulse, I just put my wet fingertips to the tips of these fingers — so that she got some water from me, and then I saw it was Mary. We looked at each other and blessed ourselves. And I realized in that moment that I loved her just as much as I had when she sat next to me in school. And outside the church she just tucked her arm in mine, and it seemed the next thing we're sitting side by side, up front, on top of the tramcar, out to Halliwell, making for the moors — the sun shining and the breeze blowing in our faces.

**Visitor** They should never have done away with the old open-topped tramcars.

**Joe** They're nice — except you get wet when it rains.

**Visitor** But think of the fresh air you get.

**Joe** Here I'll bet you must remember the old horse trams — they must have been fun.

**Visitor** Horse trams! Give over! How old do you think I am?

**Joe** Well let me see — you must have been born about eighteen — well it's hard to say, like.

**Visitor** I was born the same year as you — the same day — the same minute.

**Joe** (*To the audience*) What did I tell you! He isn't well — wandering in his mind, poor fellow. But as my mother used to say to me, never skit anybody worse off than yourself, Joe, you never know how you'll end up. (*To the Visitor*) Anyway, same as I was saying, we got off at the terminus and set off up Smithalls Dean to the moors. It was a magical day — we behaved like we were as free as air, and we could have been the only two in the world. I remember, I pinched a lovely rose out of a garden for her. I made her laugh at my jokes — she had this sort of light, happy laugh — and, of course, I brought poetry into it, and whispered a few to her.

"I was a child and she was a child,
      In this kingdom by the sea;
   But we loved with a love that was more than a love –
      I and my Annabel Lee."

Then when we'd tramped miles and miles, hand in hand. We came to a lovely grassy hollow, miles from anywhere, over Belmont. And I remember, as I stood there on the edge of it, I could smell the sea breeze coming all the way from Blackpool.

**Visitor**  You can when the wind's in the right direction. I've always
maintained you can get some of the healthiest air in the world around
Bolton.

**Joe**  Then we laid ourselves down on this lovely springy earth and
looked up to the sky. And she smelled so fragrant. I suppose living in
a house with a bathroom. After a bit, I turned and kissed her. I could
feel her young breasts against me, and her heart beating through them.
It was wonderful. I mean she kissed me like it was what she had been
longing for all her life. We never said we loved each other. I suppose
you don't have to when it's like that. She knew it and I knew it. Then
something made me put my hand on her thigh and rise up beyond —
actually, I was just showing off. But the strange thing was, she never
stopped me. The Palais girls always did — but only to coax you on
like. The next thing, I could feel the tears running down her face. The
tears were rushing silently from the corners of her eyes, down the
side of her nose, and falling on her lips. So I took my hand away and
I said, "Mary, Mary, please forgive me — I'm so sorry". She shook
her head. "There's nothing to forgive, Joe", she said. So I tried to
kiss her tears away, and she kissed me. And the next thing, we were
both crying and kissing each other. I felt that in my heart, I loved, and
would always love Mary. We stayed there on the moors until late that
evening. We caught a tram, then we cut across to her home — a big
house in Chorley New Road. And when we got there, she said, "Joe,
come in with me. I'd like you to meet my mother and father". I looked
at the house. "Please", she said. They had a large garden, and a lawn,
and rose trees, and in the house there seemed to be lights all over the
place. Somehow, at that moment, I lost my courage. She begged me to
go in, but I wouldn't. She looked so hurt and sad. I knew I'd had my
chance and missed it. Not long after that, Madge was telling me she
thought she was a week overdue. I never saw Mary again.

**Visitor**  "Last night, ah, yesternight, betwixt her lips and mine
There fell thy shadow, Cynara! Thy breath was shed
Upon my soul between the kisses and the wine;
And I was desolate and bow'd my head:
I have been faithful to thee, Cynara! in my fashion."

*A sudden sharp shunting of railway trucks is heard*

**Joe**  Crikey they've started shunting!

**Visitor**  I love that sound of coupling and uncoupling. By rights they
should never have done away with them steam engines. I mean where
are we if they cut off our oil supplies.

**Joe**  Here you'll have to excuse me, but I've got to get back to bed and
get some sleep in before the alarm goes off. I've got to go looking for
work. Not that I'll get any.

**Visitor** You might. I envy you.

**Joe** Then you must be out of your bloody mind.

**Visitor** You've got a wife, a child, a home, your health, and all your time's your own. What more do you want? Ee, but I love this place! I think it's a damn shame demolishing this row of houses.

**Joe** Demolishing!

**Visitor** Aye, to make way for the new road — joining the M something or other — connecting us with Yorkshire. Who the hell in his right mind would want connecting with Yorkshire! There was talk of putting a plaque or something outside — "Sir Joseph Eckersley lived here!" I reckon that's why the bloody Mayor voted to have the road come through. Well what else can you expect from a Liberal. (*He picks up a library book from beside the bed*) Library books, poetry — ee, I haven't had chance to read a book in years.

**Joe** I've got to go off looking for work.

**Visitor** There are more important things in this life than work.

**Joe** Not many. I need to get hold of some money — there's so much we need. A new bed, a cot, blankets, a dressing table...

**Visitor** Don't always think of what you need, Joe. Try to spare some thought for what you've got.

**Joe** We haven't had a decent meal in months. I feel hungry all the time.

**Visitor** It's hunger drives a man on.

**Joe** I've lost over a stone since I got wed!

**Visitor** I wish I could! I've just paid seventy-two pounds for a health cure and only lost half of that.

**Joe** Don't you realize we're a family living close to poverty? I want a job and a decent home.

**Visitor** Decent home! Do you think that child would be happier in a ten-guinea cot in place of that orange box? He doesn't know the difference. All he knows is the love you give him from your heart. It's bloody awful being short of money, but you'll make your way in the world all right. And you'll meet a collection of the biggest shits you've ever encountered. You'll have to become one yourself to get on. I know — I've been there. In fact I am there. I mean it Joe. I only wish I had my time over again.

*The baby cries*

**Joe** Sh, Lionel — don't be frightened — Daddy's here.

*The baby goes quiet*

**Visitor** There's a good lad.

**Joe** You know who you remind me of? My father.

**Visitor** Every man becomes his own father, Joe.

**Joe** I remember my dad would come in from the pit, feeling a bit weary perhaps, and I remember if I was crying he'd stoop down with his black face and tell me to shut up. It used to scare the daylights out of me. So that when he was washed and had his breakfast and he'd try to make it up, perhaps put me on his lap, I'd still be dead scared of him. I never got out of it. And when I was five and they told me he'd been killed in the war, it was such a relief to me to think I'd never see him again. I hope no child of mine is ever afraid of me. Do you know what they allow me for keeping him?

**Visitor** Two bob a week. You should have thought about that before you had him.

**Joe** I could cry that I can give so little to my own son.

**Visitor** Just fancy that you went down to the Labour and the chap said, "We've stopped it all".

**Joe** There'd be a bloody riot.

**Visitor** Just give him what you've got — he'll appreciate it more than you clat-arsing about what you haven't got.

**Joe** But what have I got!

**Visitor** Give him a bit of love and let him become...

**Joe** Become what?

**Visitor** Himself — what else! I mean, if you love him.

**Joe** Love him! Why this child is the greatest thing that ever happened to me!

**Visitor** Is he? As I recall, you didn't seem to think so when Madge first told you she was like that, did you?

**Joe** Well, it was a shock at the time, but I soon got over it.

**Visitor** I thought you paid a visit to that herbalist in Derby Street. A little chap with a ginger beard —. he took you into the back place to discuss it.

*Joe straightens the covering on the baby's cot*

**Joe** Well Madge wasn't quite sure at the time — she wanted——

**Visitor** He sold you a little box of pills for two-and-six.

**Joe** Yes well Madge she ——

**Visitor** And didn't you get her some gin? And then, didn't you go to one of those women, you remember...

*Joe suddenly kneels down by the cot and prays*

**Joe** Oh, God forgive me. Thank Heaven nothing at all worked.

**Visitor**  No. Madge had more sense than take 'em or visit the woman.
**Joe**  What would I have done without my little Lionel?

*Joe blesses himself and prays in a fervent whisper with stooped head and joined hands. The Visitor looks at him, not unsympathetically. Joe blesses himself again and rises to his feet*

I'm lucky, very lucky...
**Visitor**  You are that an' all. So make the best of it.

*The Visitor makes to go, but sways for a moment. Joe helps him*

**Joe**  Steady on there.
**Visitor**  I'm all right. I heard 'em saying it could turn out very serious, but it'll take more than a knock in a car to put me out. I might drop in again, just to see how you're going on.

*The Visitor goes*

*Joe looks into the cot to see if the baby is all right. He takes off his trousers and picks up the alarm clock, checks it, puts it back, and gets into bed*

**Joe**  Move over, Madge.

*Madge sighs and moves over as Joe gets down in the bed and snuggles up close to her*

*1920s music plays*

*The Lights fade*


SCENE 2

*A few minutes later*

*Lights up on a dreamy, unreal glow*

*The alarm clock is ticking. We hold the scene for some moments until the alarm clock goes off with a loud violent ring. Madge wakens first*

**Madge**  Hey the alarm! Quick! Shut it off!
**Joe**  All right... (*He wakens with a sleepy start*)

**Madge**  Shut the bloody thing off afore it wakens our Lionel.

**Joe**  I'm trying can't you see!

**Madge**  Press lever down — press it down — afore it wakens him.

**Joe**  I can't find the bloody thing.

*Joe upsets the bowl and alarm clock and they fall to the floor. The baby starts crying*

**Madge**  (*with a light and good natured undertone*) You great numb sod! You've done it now. (*She gets out of bed and goes to quieten the baby*)

**Joe**  Let me pick him up.

**Madge**  You stay where you are a minute and be told — I'll rock cot. Sh! Sh! It'll send him off. (*She picks the baby up and cuddles him and he stops crying*) Come on — come on — that's enough of that — upsy-tupsy — there, there, there.

*Joe manages to shut the alarm off and picks up the clock to listen*

**Joe**  Thank God it's still going. I thought I'd busted it.

**Madge**  You might as well for what flaming use all that din is every morning. Why do you have to put the clock in the flamin' tin bowl?

**Joe**  To make sure I hear it.

**Madge**  You could hear that din on Rivington Pike.

**Joe**  Then why didn't we hear it yesterday?

**Madge**  Because it never went off. You'll have Mrs Worthington knocking on the wall again.

**Joe**  I can't help that. I've got to get up to go out looking see can I get a start at work, haven't I? (*He starts dressing*)

**Madge**  But you know there's no work to be had.

**Joe**  Of course I know it. And with millions out of work, it's not likely they'd pick on me.

**Madge**  Then what's the use of you getting out of your warm bed — pedalling a couple of miles in all that rain and fog, and standing at the coal-yard gate waiting for a day's work you know you'll never get?

**Joe**  Because it might stop some folk from talking.

**Madge**  If you mean my mam.

**Joe**  How did you guess!

**Madge**  She said you don't push yourself forward enough that were all.

**Joe**  You can tell your mother from me that the only time I pushed myself forward, I've had cause to regret.

**Madge**  What exactly do you mean by that, Joe Eckersley?

**Joe**  Nothing. And what about your father?

**Madge** He only said you won't go out of your way to please folk — like that time he put you a good word in with my Uncle Percy for that job at the railway, and you ——

**Joe** I've never been a bum-licker, and I don't propose to be one now — not if I never get a job.

**Madge** Folk have to do a lot of things they never did, to keep going these days.

**Joe** Well I'm not. And you can tell your father I'm not joining none of his bloody clubs, the British Legion and all the rest of it.

**Madge** It's just the British Legion takes an interest in you.

**Joe** Why the hell should they take an interest in me? I wasn't in the war.

**Madge** No but your dad were. And he got killed.

**Joe** D'you think I want them to find me a job just because they got my father blown to bits?

**Madge** All right, Joe. I'm sorry.

**Joe** I'll show 'em, one day. I'll not be beholden to any bloody one of 'em. If only I'd a few quid in my pocket, I'd tell 'em what I thought of 'em.

**Madge** They meant no harm, Joe. Try not to take the things folk say too seriously. My mam and dad think the world of you and you know that.

**Joe** I'm not sure they do.

**Madge** They know you're just looking round for the right job.

**Joe** I'm looking for any damn job. Anyway, one day I'll pay 'em back treble anything we've ever had from them. I vow that. If I had my way I'd never go out of the house except to go to the library — I can occupy myself just thinking and reading library books. I'd as soon come across a line of poetry as took me fancy than all your bloody jobs.

**Madge** We can't live on poetry. (*To the baby*) Rest you there, Lionel, whilst Mum and Dad have their little sleep out.

*Madge turns and goes back to bed. Joe watches her as she plumps up the pillows and makes room for him*

**Joe** What do you mean little sleep out? I'm not going back to bed.

**Madge** Why not? You always like an extra five minutes. You say it's worth all your other night's sleep.

**Joe** I've got my trousers on!

**Madge** You can always take 'em off again. It wouldn't be the first time.

**Joe** I'm going down to the coal-yard to see if I can get a start at work! What do you think I set the alarm for?

**Madge**  You know what happens when you get up in a rush and go
dashing off — you get one of your migraine headaches. Your mother
warned me about that.

**Joe**  Aye and I know what happens when I come back to bed with you.

**Madge**  It doesn't have to happen does it?

**Joe**  No but somehow it always does.

**Madge**  It takes two to make a bargain. Besides I hope you've got some
willpower left.

**Joe**  Willpower, for God's sake!

**Madge**  Then put your mind on something else. Just think of the
Wanderers winning the Cup or the fun you'll have when you're dead.

**Joe**  How can I keep my mind on something else? There's a feeling in a
man and it seems to dominate him from the age of five until they carry
him off. When I feel your warm naked backside ——

**Madge**  Joe! Language!

**Joe**  I've said nothing.

**Madge**  I don't like that word "naked". It's suggestive.

**Joe**  I was saying what it does to me when I feel your — a saint couldn't
resist it.

**Madge**  What's all this talk about resist?

**Joe**  And I've never got over the feeling it's a sin. I mean, even though
we're married.

**Madge**  What's a sin?

**Joe**  You wouldn't understand proper, not being a Catholic, so I don't
mention it in case I'd spoil things for you.

**Madge**  You won't spoil anything for me. What's a sin?

**Joe**  You know, all this lighthearted intercourse. It seems too good for
this life.

**Madge**  Lighthearted intercourse! Well, I could always come over that
bit solemn, like, if it would ease your conscience for you. God knows,
it's little enough pleasure you get these days. And it's not as if you
went about it like a maniac. I mean, you've grown very loving, Joe,
and you do like your kiss and a joke along the way.

**Joe**  Wait until I come back.

**Madge**  It's not as though it were rationed. After all, you're a long time
dead.

**Joe**  I haven't the time — look at that clock.

**Madge**  The clock is fast.

**Joe**  Aye but only ten minutes.

**Madge**  I put it on an extra quarter of an hour last night when you were
out back. And it does gain a bit. So you've at least twenty-five minutes
to fill in.

**Joe**  I wish you wouldn't egg me on.

**Madge**  I can't bear to think of you going out into the world in a hot,
unsatisfied state like.

*Madge makes room for Joe*

**Joe**  I soon cool down once I get out in the rain.

**Madge**  Besides, you should consider yourself lucky. The postman's wife told me she always charges him. She's got a savings box under the bed and she makes him put a shilling in every time.

**Joe**  I don't fancy he'll spend all that much.

**Madge**  She reckons it all but pays for their holidays.

**Joe**  Twenty-five minutes did you say?

**Madge**  About twenty-two now. You've wasted three minutes standing there.

**Joe**  I wonder, ought I to leave my trousers on?

**Madge**  You mean get into bed with your trousers on?

**Joe**  They would be a bit of protection.

**Madge**  Ee, but I wouldn't altogether fancy lying in bed beside a chap with his hands in his pockets. I don't think it's dignified for one thing. Then suppose what you fear never — and you found yourself in bed with your pants on — the next thing you might say to yourself, "What the heck have I got these things on for!" And that could very well put the one thing you're trying so hard to forget back into your mind. Do you follow what I'm saying?

**Joe**  Not properly, but if I come back in with you, I've definitely got to have something to put me off. There's no holding me of late. It's getting out of hand. I find myself standing at that coal-yard like a chap hypnotised. I lost a day's work last week when one chap behind stepped in ahead of me.

**Madge**  Here, I know what — they say thinking of his worries puts a man off, so you take off your trousers, Joe, and come into bed and have a nice rest, and I'll keep reminding you of all your worries, and you'll get up refreshed.

**Joe**  Well, I suppose there's no point in standing like this for the next twenty minutes. I might as well risk it. Life seems one trial after another.

*Madge invitingly holds the blankets open. Joe takes off his trousers and tentatively gets into bed*

**Madge**  That's better than standing isn't it?

**Joe**  Ooh, doesn't it smell warm?

**Madge**  How do you mean "Doesn't it smell warm?"

**Joe**  It smells warm like, here in bed.

**Madge**  Oh, I see. I wasn't quite sure what you meant at first — the way you said it.

**Joe** Don't come too near, Madge, you know how Jo-Jo is — worries or no worries.

**Madge** I won't go near him. It can't be pleasant for my little Jo-Jo, standing up like that hours on end.

**Joe** He seems to know when there's nothing doing

**Madge** I'll see he doesn't get out of hand.

**Joe** Madge...!

**Madge** I'm not anywhere near you! I'm over the other side of the bed. Just look!

**Joe** Well you feel near.

**Madge** It's all right, Joe, don't worry. I'll keep over my side. Have you got yourself nice and comfy? Right, now about all your troubles... (*She holds up her hand and ticks the troubles off on her fingers*) One, come this Friday, we'll be exactly three weeks behind with the rent.

**Joe** I've been worried about that rent. We don't want turning out. We must get straight up one way or another.

**Madge** We'll get straight, Joe, once you get a start.

**Joe** Madge, mind where you touch me.

**Madge** I'm not touching you! They could put another couple between us. Besides, you've got your underpants on haven't you?

**Joe** Yes but I find a pair of cotton underpants with holes in is not much defence.

**Madge** Now let me see, where was we? Oh yes, the rent — and now, the back window — we need a new pane of glass for that. Ee, my feet are cold. They feel frozen.

**Joe** All right, you can put 'em on me. But mind where. It's really the landlord's job.

**Madge** What is?

**Joe** That back window.

**Madge** Oh, I see.

**Joe** It was cracked when we came in.

**Madge** I don't mind that piece of plywood. It fits, that's the main thing.

**Joe** Yes but it doesn't let much light through.

**Madge** I were just saying...

**Joe** And mind where you're warming them.

**Madge** They might cool you down. They don't bring you on, do they dear?

**Joe** You know how it always ends up when I trim your toenails. I don't get time to get my thumb out of the scissors. You've got wonderful feet, Madge.

**Madge** It comes from wearing clogs from birth. But, come to think of it, it's quite romantic really, having your husband trim your toenails by gaslight. Beats all your going to the pictures!

**Joe** Remember last Friday night? I didn't even get down to your left foot!

**Madge**  No, you can trim that one this Friday night! I think you'd make a fortune if you ever set up as a chiropodist.

**Joe**  I don't want to be late at the gates, in case there's a job going. You can earn nine bob a day coal-bagging. We'd soon clear off all our debts. Get enough glass for the whole bloody house.

**Madge**  Ooh, that's better. How you keep so warm I don't know!

**Joe**  How you get so flamin' cold I don't know!

**Madge**  You've got such lovely skin for a man, Joe.

**Joe**  You know, Madge, you look your best at mornings. Sort of nice and rested. It brings out your good looks.

**Madge**  Ah well, you want something to look at if you've nowt to eat.

**Joe**  You've got a lovely warm smell too.

**Madge**  Isn't it nice to think that there's nowt the Prince of Wales can do in bed that we can't.

**Joe**  The Prince of Wales is a bachelor. He's only supposed to sleep when he goes to bed.

**Madge**  Well, the Aga Khan, and Solly Joel, and all that lot with money.

**Joe**  I'd rather stick to my own cabbage patch and make no comparisons.

**Madge**  Yes, I expect they've all got their own problems.

**Joe**  Excuse me, you're getting a bit close, yu'know...

**Madge**  Oh, sorry!

**Joe**  I'd best get up, while I've still got the determination.

**Madge**  I tell you, you're all right. I know you better than you know yourself. What do you keep fretting yourself for? Relax!

**Joe**  I think it's starting.

**Madge**  It might be a false alarm. Let me have a feel.

**Joe**  Ho, no, no, don't Madge!

**Madge**  Why? What's up?

**Joe**  That's the worst thing you can do. You know how he is. You know what he does when he feels your hand.

**Madge**  I thought perhaps, if I patted him once or twice, he might go off to sleep. Shall I make sure?

**Joe**  No! No! No don't, Madge, don't! Whatever you do! (*He sits up slightly*)

**Madge**  All right, I won't. But don't let it scare you — rest back a minute! Now, where was we?

**Joe**  Were!

**Madge**  What?

**Joe**  Where were we?

**Madge**  Oh yes. I'm afraid the coal won't last out the week.

**Joe**  I might pick up a half a hundredweight from the coal-yard — when I get my dole on Friday.

**Madge** We was up to the milkman — I didn't pay him last week. And that far wall needs plastering. The corner shop——

**Joe** Eh?

**Madge** — won't let us have much more on the slate. Is it working?

**Joe** Aye, but don't overdo things. It might easy go into reverse. You know, the more the worries, the less use fighting against them.

**Madge** It could be worse if it were t'other way around. And I'm behind with the clothing club payments. And there's the back bedroom ceiling. Y'know what I'm beginning to enjoy this lot...

**Joe** Madge, I'm afraid ——

**Madge** Don't be afraid, love — if the worst comes to the worst, we're entitled to, what they call it — y'know — consummation.

**Joe** We consummated it all a very long time ago.

**Madge** And I hope we can go on consummating it. Until we're ninety. We're married — both in the eyes of God and the law, and they can't take it away!

**Joe** I don't think anybody wants to take it away. I just like to exert some self-control before I go looking for work. There it goes again! Didn't you feel it?

**Madge** I felt nothing untoward. Except — well, to be frank, I thought it was your jumpy knee or something.

**Joe** It starts lower down. I'm sick and fed up with it. Nature gives a chap no peace!

**Madge** Poor little Jo-Jo. Funny how he's either plaguing the life out of you or you're plaguing it out of him. Perhaps you should give him his head a bit more.

**Joe** If I were to give him his head a bit more, I'd *never* get out of this flamin' bed. There's only this thin line between a normal man and a sex maniac. If I were to abandon myself to it...

**Madge** I see what you mean. You don't think we should try it out?

**Joe** Yes, but not now. Besides, have you noticed how I go lately — my heart thudding away?

**Madge** You've become more passionate since we got married.

**Joe** That's not passion, that's weakness, and I break into a sweat as well.

**Madge** What's a drop of sweat between husband and wife? I think you're one of the great lovers, Joe.

**Joe** A funny thing — but of late, I seem to have taken to floating, y'know.

**Madge** Floating? How do you mean?

**Joe** Well, at the big moment — you know — it seems as if I start floating round the room.

**Madge** Ee, I'll have to keep an eye on you, love. I wouldn't like you to bang your head on the ceiling. Suppose I got up and put your trousers on and got back into bed with them? By the way is it working better now you're sitting up?

**Joe** I'm not sure. He's gone quiet.

**Madge** Good. Then you don't want me to do what I did on the train coming back from Blackpool that time do you? That worked like magic.

**Joe** What! Not blooming likely! Ooh, I'll never forget it!

**Madge** But it was you said squeeze him.

**Joe** Yes, but I'd forgot you'd been a bobbin-carrier. I couldn't walk proper for a month.

**Madge** I only did what I was told.

**Joe** At times, Madge, you seem to forget he's attached to me.

**Madge** Oh, I know what, Joe. Let me huddle up to you and you recite a poem.

**Joe** Eh?

**Madge** Like you did one Saturday night in our backstreet. When you were playing football on the Sunday and wanted to save your energy. It worked then.

**Joe** It's a pity I didn't recite poems every bloody night.

**Madge** Now don't you be cheeky! There were one called "The Slave's Dream". I like that. What's up now?

**Joe** Madge, you know what I often wish? I wish I'd been first there with you.

**Madge** How many more times do I have to tell you, you were the first and the only one! I've never loved anyone but you.

**Joe** I'm not talking about love. But let's not start an argument. "The Slave's Dream" by Henry Wadsworth Longfellow.

**Madge** "Beside the ungather'd rice he lay,
        His sickle in his hand..."

**Joe** You what?

**Madge** I were just starting you off.

**Joe** I don't need starting off.
        "His breast was bare,
        His matted hair was buried in the sand."
    Keep your bottom away from me, Madge!

**Madge** Oh, pardon me, I didn't realize. It's on account of where the bed sags. How's that? Now you can carry on. But don't bring up that other daft idea again. You like to torture yourself.

**Joe** Let's shut up about it.
        "Again in the mist and shadow of sleep,
        He saw his native land.
        Wide through the landscape of his dreams,
        The lordly Niger flowed:
        Beneath the palm-trees on the plain..."
    Keep it away when I tell you!

**Madge** Sorry I slipped.

**Joe**   "Once more a king he strode;
     And heard the tinkling caravans
     Descend the mountain-road.
     He saw once more his dark-eyed queen."
  It's not working!

**Madge**   Try to keep your mind on the slave. Now go on.
     "He saw once more his dark-eyed queen..."

**Joe**   *(working up to a furious speed)*
     "Among her children stand:
     They clasp'd his neck, they kiss'd his cheeks
     They held him by the hand!
     A tear burst from the sleeper's lids
     And fell into the sand.
     And then at furious speed he rode
     Along the Niger's bank;
     His bridle reins were golden chains,
     And, with a martial clank,
     At each leap he could feel his scabbard of steel..."
  Madge, it's getting the upper hand on me! *(Breathless, loud, bursting)*
     "Smiting his stallion's flank.
     Before him, like a blood-red flag,
     The bright flamingos flew..."
  It's no flaming use! *(He leaps out of bed)*

**Madge**   What's up with you?

**Joe**   What do you think?

*Joe does three or four swift toe-touching bends, arms stretched from above his head, with Madge watching him as though he were mad*

**Madge**   What the hell are you doing now?

**Joe**   Exercises. They're the best thing for taking your mind off.

**Madge**   You could have had it all over and done with by this time.

*Joe nimbly gets into a position with his shoulders on the floor and starts "bicycling" energetically*

**Joe**   I wish we had a bath. I'd have a right cold bath. I'd love that.

**Madge**   I feel sorry for you, Joe Eckersley, to be plagued with a thing like that! I do honest. I'd go and fling myself in the canal, I would...

*Joe stops bicycling for a moment*

**Joe**   No need to feel all that sorry! It's natural in a normal fellow. There's men going around would give their bottom dollar to get a touch of that. It's not a bloody disease, you know!

**Madge**  No, but anybody'd think it were the way you go on. Why, if you'd had any sense, you could have been floating round the room by now. (*To the audience*) If he's right in the head, I'm not.

*Madge grabs the army topcoat and goes*

*Joe continues exercising*

*The Visitor enters*

**Visitor**  You were cheating, Joe. Bending at the knees.

**Joe**  Eh?

**Visitor**  You're a bit out of puff. Not bad though. All you need is a good steak or two. Have you still got a sex problem, Joe?

**Joe**  My only problem is that I enjoy it too much.

**Visitor**  Where's she gone?

**Joe**  Something seems to have upset her. I can't think what. Women are funny buggers. You never know when you have 'em.

**Visitor**  What did you get out of bed for?

**Joe**  I have to go looking for a job.

**Visitor**  You're not looking for a job now. What I wouldn't give for a chance like that you've just turned down.

**Joe**  Well, I must be going. I want to get a start. I've got to think of the future.

**Visitor**  Make the most of now. Life slips by whilst you're thinking of what life will be like.

**Joe**  Make the most of what?

**Visitor**  Your youth and your young blood. What happens at your age is that you find yourself looking forward to life — then at my age you find yourself looking back. And you wonder where the hell it got to. It's like eating a boiled egg with no yolk. You're hoping to come across it every spoonful until you hit the bottom of the shell and realize there isn't going to be any. Love that child, your son. Love that woman, your wife.

**Joe**  But that woman isn't the one I really love.

**Visitor**  I know. Mary Carlisle. There was that wonderful Sunday. The walk across the moors.

**Joe**  The way she cried.

**Visitor**  Lying down beside her on the springy heather.

**Joe**  I'll never forget it.

**Visitor**  I know that, Joe, but love Madge just the same.

**Joe**  In a way I'd like to.

**Visitor**  Except you won't let yourself. You like to imagine yourself in love with someone you haven't got, to save yourself giving real love to someone you have.

**Joe**  You wouldn't by any chance know the man she went with before
me — I mean the man who was there first?
**Visitor**  You're not jealous are you?
**Joe**  What?
**Visitor**  Jealousy comes from not loving somebody. Love her. That's the
answer. Look at her. She's beautiful. What was it that Keats said?
**Joe**      "Beauty is truth, truth beauty..."
**Visitor**  No not that. The other...
**Joe**      "A thing of beauty is a joy forever.
              Its loveliness increases..."
**Visitor**  That's the one.
              "Its loveliness increases,
              It will never pass into nothingness."
Have you got that Joe?
              "It will never pass into nothingness."

*1920s music plays*

*The Lights fade*

# ACT II

## SCENE 1

*The kitchen*

*A few minutes later*

*There is a bare morning greyness about the scene. The kitchen is gaslit. It has an old-fashioned range, with hob, oven, and a fender in front. The baby's napkins hang over a clothes-horse. Joe's jacket is hanging over the back of a chair. The furniture, though poor, has a homely look. There is a low slopstone (or sink). The alarm clock is prominent. There is a suggestion of warmth, and the feeling comes through, that whatever it looks like, the people in it like and enjoy the place*

*Madge is wearing the army topcoat over the old shirt of Joe's. She is filling the kettle at the tap and putting it on the hob. She takes a two-ounce packet of tea from a tin that serves as a tea-caddy. The packet is obviously almost empty and she tips the contents into a pint mug. She takes the bottom of the packet apart to make sure she gets the last tea-leaf out. Then she takes up a blue sugar bag and it is obvious that this too is almost empty. She scrapes round the inside of it with a spoon and puts the sugar in the pint pot, then takes the bag to pieces and carefully coaxes the last few grains out and into the pot.*

*Joe enters from the yard, wheeling his bicycle. He has on his shirt with the sleeves rolled up, trousers, old working boots, waistcoat, scarf tucked in it, and a cap. He wheels the bicycle through the kitchen. He sets it up and feels the tyre.*

**Joe** I thought I'd got a slow puncture but I think it's all right.
**Madge** If I were you I'd pump it up.

*Joe removes the pump, fits the connector and screws on the valve. Then he bends down to start pumping. After a moment or two, he stops and Madge looks up*

**Joe** I'm not sure why my pump's not working.

**Madge** Oh well keep on trying.

*Joe removes pump and examines it, giving it a few sharp pumps*

**Joe** It could be a bit of grit in the pipe, or it might be the valve.
**Madge** Or you might have a faulty connector. You haven't a penny for
the gas have you?

*Joe feels in all his pockets*

**Joe** You shouldn't have really bothered getting up, Madge.
**Madge** I don't like to see you going out on an empty stomach. Besides,
I didn't fancy just lying there.

*Joe at last finds the penny and gives it to Madge*

Ta, Joe.
**Joe** You're welcome.
**Madge** I'm glad you're not one of these husbands who hates parting. I
mean with money.
**Joe** I only wish I'd more to part with.
**Madge** You didn't want it for anything, did you — I mean, a smoke?
**Joe** I was saving tuppence for a five packet of Woodbines.
**Madge** There's a threepenny bit I can let you have.
**Joe** No, I wouldn't take the housekeeping money if I never had a
smoke.

*Madge crosses to Joe and kisses him*

**Madge** You're not a bad old pig, Joe. I'd make you a sauce butty if we
had any bread, only we've no sauce.
**Joe** I'm not all that hungry.

*Joe starts pumping up the bicycle tyre. Madge knocks the bottom of an
almost empty sauce bottle with her palm, onto a slice of bread*

**Madge** Hey, you're lucky — I've dug you up a crust and squeezed you
a few blobs out.
**Joe** (*still stooped down, feeling at the tyre*) Eh?
**Madge** Mind you don't get the blood settling in your head!
**Madge** By the way did it work? I mean your exercises and that.
**Joe** Madge!
**Madge** It's funny when you put it off.

**Joe**  When you put what off?

**Madge**  Same as we've just done. Put it off like. It seems to go to your mind.

**Joe**  I wish you wouldn't hark back.

**Madge**  All right, Joe love. Here, sup your tea — it's all milked and sugared and I brewed it in the pint pot — I think it holds the flavour better.

**Joe**  Ta.

*Joe puts down pump and takes the mug from Madge. He has a drink and she gives him the sauce butty. He takes a bite*

Here, have a bite.

*Madge takes a bite and kisses Joe. Joe gives Madge the mug. He puts away the pump and starts to put on his jacket*

**Madge**  (*examining the tea-leaves*). According to your tea-leaves you'll be coming into some money.

**Joe**  Well I could do with some! *(Pause)* I keep getting this funny feeling I might get a start today.

**Madge**  You've got no end of funny feelings lately. Will there be many waiting at the gate for work?

**Joe**  Aye, happen a dozen. It's all according. Oh, I knew there was something I forgot to tell you — you know who turned up there yesterday looking for work? Gussy — Gussy Davis!

**Madge**  You mean Gussy the Waltz?

**Joe**  Aye. Little Gussy. Front of the queue. Must have stayed up all night Couldn't keep still. Hopping from toe to toe he was.

**Madge**  Happen he was cold.

**Joe**  He was wearing his old navy blue suit — couldn't have kept much cold out. He reckoned he'd had a feed of ham and eggs for breakfast.

**Madge**  How the hell could he get bacon and eggs on the dole? He's never smelt bacon for months.

**Joe**  Says his wife can spin the money out!

**Madge**  The same old Gussy.

**Joe**  He says, "We've got to get jobs — country can't afford to keep us all in idleness. It'll go bankrupt" .

**Madge**  It'll not go bankrupt on what it's giving my family.

**Joe**  It riles me the way he shows off.

**Madge**  He's not really a brag — it's more innocence than anything. But he were a beautiful dancer.

**Joe**  No good at owt else.

**Madge** Better than any professional.

**Joe** Yes, I'll admit he was quite a fair waltzer, but I was always his daddy at the tango.

**Madge** Oh yes, without a doubt! Nobody could touch you at the tango. He once asked me to have the last waltz with him — and it was like a dream dance — I'll never forget it.

*Madge begins to waltz dreamily, and hum* Ramona. *Joe sees Madge dancing and looks at her somewhat amazed. Madge stops*

I'd a feeling life would never again be the same for me after that waltz.

**Joe** I never knew Gussy Davis got to dance with you.

**Madge** It were before I knew you. I mean, I used to admire you from the distance. It were one Saturday night of the holiday week. All the Palais clique were away in Blackpool. I expect you were there too. When he came over and asked me, I couldn't believe my own ears. I were only a learner you might say.

**Joe** You would be.

**Madge** They were all jealous of me, all the other girls. But what a dancer. Thank God I've always been good at following. So he got married did he?

**Joe** Yes. His dancing days are over now. He's got twins about a twelve month old and another on the way. That's why he's so anxious to work.

**Madge** He seemed born to dance — but not to marry.

**Joe** Hey, it's nearly time I was off!

*Madge comes up to Joe and gives a wifely touch of buttoning Joe's jacket up and pulling his scarf more tightly across his chest. She kisses him*

**Madge** Joe, do you er...?

**Joe** What?

**Madge** You know — do you love me...? Tell me honest.

**Joe** Course I love you. What a time to ask!

**Madge** I thought it as good as any — just as you were about to kiss me. There are times when I get the feeling I'm only here on sufferance. On account of the baby like. I mean, if I hadn't got into trouble, you'd never have married me.

**Joe** Of course I would — perhaps not as sudden but I'd have got round to it in time. I've got to be off — kiss...?

*Joe kisses Madge lightly*

**Madge** I'll tell you what I sometimes feel — I sometimes feel when you kiss me, you've got that other girl behind your mind.

**Joe** What other girl?

**Madge** The one you went a walk with that Easter Sunday — you left me standing by the Ram's Head waiting for you for hours, and you never turned up — Mary something-or-other.

**Joe** Now, Madge, haven't I told you not to bring her name up?

**Madge** Why, what is it about her that's so different from anybody else?

**Joe** Just keep her out of it that's all. And what about you, eh? What about him as had a go at you before me? Who was he? You won't tell me that will you?

**Madge** Oh, we're not having that flaming record on again are we? At half past six in the morning? If I'm not ——

**Joe** You started it and I'll finish it. I know somebody did.

**Madge** I've told you till I'm sick of telling you, you were the first there with me, Joe Eckersley.

**Joe** I was not! I know I wasn't.

**Madge** You were! I tell you I were a virgin until that Saturday night.

**Joe** Some bloody virgin...!

**Madge** You'd have known I were, if you knew anything about that sort of thing.

**Joe** Madge, love, listen do tell me, please — I won't be angry, I promise — it's just to set my mind at rest. It maggots me. I can't sleep at nights.

**Madge** But I've told you, Joe, there were nobody. Nobody but you. Anyway, of what importance can it be to you now one way or t'other?

**Joe** Don't you see, it's exactly those things that plague a man?

**Madge** Well I tell you, you were the first.

*Joe grabs Madge*

**Joe** You bloody liar! You once admitted I wasn't when you lost your temper that New Year's Eve. But you wouldn't say who. Now who the hell was he? Out with it now!

**Madge** Let go of me!

**Joe** I will when you tell me. Who was it? I must know!

*Madge breaks free*

**Madge** I tell you you were first. First and only one!

**Joe** Why did you say there had been someone?

**Madge** I only said it to satisfy your nasty mind. I made it up. And what about that bloody Mary, eh? What about her?

**Joe**  Ssh, don't shout, Madge — the neighbours, they'll hear you!

**Madge**  I don't care who hears me. What about you, eh? You and that Mary?

**Joe**  Sh!

**Madge**  You once called her name out in your sleep.

**Joe**  I did not!

**Madge**  Yes you did, I heard you.

**Joe**  Now I'm telling you, if you bring her name up again...

**Madge**  Why, is she too flaming precious?

**Joe**  I don't see what you're so jealous about. I've told you I never touched her. I could swear it on my oath.

**Madge**  Swear it on your oath! Don't you see, that's just what I am jealous about? You could have poked her uphill and down bloody dale for all I care — it might have got her out of your system. But no, you never touched her— you'd too much respect for your Mary! But you touched me all right, didn't you! Just because I loved you, and I'd let you do anything to me. And you never realized all it meant to me — never even said you loved me.

**Joe**  Oh, I did, Madge! More than once.

**Madge**  Not on that first night you didn't. I had to drag it out of you, on our way home.

**Joe**  To be honest, I think I must have gone kind of dizzy or something that night in the stone quarry, Madge. I've never known a feeling like it, before or since. I felt sort of transported. And at the same time I'd this half fear something might fall on me from above.

**Madge**  I sometimes wish something had, sooner than you carry on like this. But don't think I don't know what's behind it all.

**Joe**  What? What's behind it?

**Madge**  And don't think I didn't know what was going on in your mind all the time — you thought I were common — cheap and common — just because I worked in the mill.

**Joe**  That's not true!

**Madge**  Oh yes, it is! And happen I smelt of it, eh? Of oil and cotton and the cardroom. I loved you that much I could refuse you nothing, but you kept all your bloody highfalutin' thoughts for that Mary!

*A loud knocking is heard on the wall*

**Joe**  What did I tell you! That's Mrs Worthington knocking on the wall! I knew she would!

**Madge**  To hell with Missis Worthington!

**Joe**  God knows how much she's heard.

**Madge**  It's our home isn't it?

**Joe**  The next thing, all the street will know.

**Madge** I don't care what they know.

**Joe** Sorry, Mrs Worthington — it won't happen again. And my mother warned us not to go antagonising the neighbours. You never know when you need them.

**Madge** And to hell with your mother too.

**Joe** Madge, love, let me wipe your eyes.

*Joe wipes Madge's eyes*

**Madge** S'all right, I'll be all right.

**Joe** I do respect you, Madge. I respect you more every day I live with you, because I find new things to respect. And I'll never forget how good you were when you were carrying our Lionel. And you'd so little to eat.

**Madge** Don't talk daft, Joe.

**Joe** And how brave you were when he was being born. You hardly let out a squeak. You've more in you than I'll ever have.

**Madge** I'm nothing and nobody. It's only I'd feel so lonely if I thought you loved anyone else more than me.

**Joe** But I don't.

**Madge** Because I love you, and I've given all I have to you. And I can't imagine anybody else but you.

**Joe** But of course I love you.

**Madge** Some nights when we've made love and you turn away after I ——

**Joe** I tell you, I love you.

**Madge** Let me finish. When you turn away ——

**Joe** I don't turn away on purpose. I turn away just to cool off. Madge, I'm sorry. I'll have to be off now or it'll be no use going.

**Madge** Let me finish. I wonder, are you thinking of her.

**Joe** Of course I'm not.

**Madge** I couldn't bear it if you were.

*Joe kisses Madge with passion*

**Joe** Madge, I'll have to be off now.

**Madge** Nob'dy would ever know if you didn't go waiting for work.

**Joe** I know, but it keeps me straight with myself.

**Madge** Suppose you get a start at work?

**Joe** I'll get a start when Nelson gets his flamin' eye back. The minute all the horse carters and coal-baggers are in and the gaffer shouts, "nothing doing" I'll hop back on my bike and belt like mad home again.

**Madge** I'll have you a nice warm breakfast ready when you get back. I've got an egg for you and a streaky rasher. I got them from my mam yesterday, but I were keeping it a secret.

**Joe**  What have I told you about taking things from your mother! You
know I'd sooner starve than ask anybody for anything.

**Madge**  I promised her I'd eat 'em and say nowt to you. Course, I could
make dipped butties with a bit of egg and bacon on — and we'd take
'em to bed with us. That might turn out right nice.

*Madge nestles up to Joe and he puts his arm around her*

Ee, but I feel sorry for other women who live round here. They seem
to have no romance in their lives, like you and me. I wonder what
happens to it all.

**Joe**  Think something else up to surprise me will you. You know, in love
like.

**Madge**  Yes, anything you want, Joe. I'm yours. All yours.

*Joe and Madge kiss hard*

**Joe**  Something like you did last Sunday morning.

**Madge**  What was that? Oh — you've got to be in the mood for that — it
sort of came out by accident — won't you think bad of me.

**Joe**  Course I won't.

**Madge**  I'm always afraid you will. I don't know what gets into me at
times.

*They kiss again*

**Joe**  It was lovely, Madge, it was honest. You've got more than any film
star, Theda Bara and the rest of them.

*Joe kisses her lightly*

**Joe**  See you about quarter to eight.

*Joe begins to wheel his bicycle to the door*

**Madge**  Leave it to me. I'll have everything ready.

**Joe**  Right that's a promise.

**Madge**  You never said your morning prayer like you do.

*Joe stands with his bike beside the door and closes his eyes and blesses
himself. Madge joins hands with him, unsurely*

**Joe**  My God, I offer thee — one day, Madge, I'll make up to you for all
this — I offer thee all the prayers, works and sufferings of this day. I'll

see you have a lovely home — everything you need — and I beseech thee to give me Thy grace that I may not offend Thee this day. But faithfully serve Thee and do Thy holy will in all things. Amen.

**Madge** I've got everything I need now. I've got you and I've got our Lionel. And what if we're a bit hungry betimes, we've got other things folk with fat bellies might envy. When I'm by myself, washing at the slopstone or bathing our Lionel, I often thank God, and beg him to look after us, and never let us separate.

*Joe kisses Madge*

**Joe** Well, goodbye.
**Madge** Oh, aren't we happy, Joe!
**Joe** We're not too bad.

*Joe starts to wheel his bike out*

**Joe** Christ, it's a bloody wet morning!
**Madge** Go careful — mind you don't run your bike int' tramlines. God speed, Joe. I'll be waiting for you, like I said.

*Joe exits*

*1920s music plays*

*The Lights fade*

SCENE 2

*The kitchen*

*Evening of the same day*

*We hear Gene Austin singing "My Blue Heaven". The scene has a warm and cosy evening glow. The baby's cot has been placed on a chair and a stool. A clothes-horse stands in front of stove with napkins and baby clothes airing. There is a large saucepan on the hob*

*Madge is wearing a freshly ironed blouse and dark skirt, and she looks attractive. The baby gives a cry*

**Madge** Now, now, Lionel, hush up! I know you've missed Daddy, but he'll be home soon. He won't be too long now love. We must have everything nice for him when he gets home.

*Madge picks up a newspaper and starts to lay it on the table, smoothing it carefully as though it were a real cloth. She takes cutlery from the drawer in the table and begins to lay places for herself and Joe, talking to the baby throughout. Her manner has taken on a brisk house-wifely confidence*

I never thought he'd get taken on! They must have been short of men. There were daft me, sitting up in bed with two dipped egg and bacon butties. I don't know how we're going to stick it if he ever gets a full time job. It's so lonely without him. But he had to earn pennies to buy you a pram. (*She goes to the oven and looks in*) Oh, I think it's nearly done. (*She leaves oven door open and puts a kitchen towel to dry over it. Then she crosses to the window to look and see whether Joe is coming*) No sign of him yet, love. (*She picks up a hand mirror*) I must calm down. I'm getting all hot and bothered. Ee, I've forgotten his slippers. (*She picks up an old pair of patent leather dancing shoes*) He could fairly Charleston in these. Ee, I sometimes wonder, did we cut off his youth a bit too soon, poor beggar.

*The clatter of the bicycle is heard outside*

Ee, Lionel, I think your father's here now! Won't he be glad to see you! (*She hurriedly tidies herself*) Are you back then?

*Joe stumbles in with the bicycle. Stiff and weary, he is hardly recognizable from the chirpy chap who left that morning. His face is black from coal-dust, clothes are soaked with rain. He wheels the bicycle out into the back yard*

*Madge has a warm greeting on her lips and she half holds her face forward for a kiss but Joe seems not to see her*

**Madge**  Oh Joe, love, what a wet — oh, I'm so glad — I say isn't it...?

*Madge stares after Joe, bewildered. Joe slowly re-enters. He goes to the tap and takes a drink of water from a cup. Madge watches. Joe takes off his cap and lets it drop. Then he begins to struggle out of his wet jacket and scarf. Madge, a little late, hurries to help him take his jacket off*

I'll just let 'em drip.

*Madge busies herself hanging the wet clothes up, spreading newspaper to catch the drips. Joe slowly sits down on the fender stool like a man who is stiff and can hardly move. His shirt is torn and his arms are black from rain and coal-dust. Madge can't understand what has happened*

Can I get you anything?

*Joe doesn't answer. Madge feels at a loss, then tries again*

I've made you a potato pie...

*Joe still doesn't answer*

Will you have it now or later?

**Joe**  I'm not hungry
**Madge**  There's meat, an' onions, an' everything in it — just like you like it.
**Joe**  I'm not hungry.
**Madge**  But ——
**Joe**  I tell you, I don't want any. I feel shagged.

*Madge looks at Joe, helplessly. The baby cries, and Madge hurries to the cot*

**Madge**  Sh, sh, love!
**Joe**  Hush him up can't you!

*Madge gets rather panicky and fussily tries to comfort the baby, but the baby cries more loudly. Joe rises to his feet and Madge looks at him a little fearfully as he walks across to the cot and looks down into it. Madge instinctively makes a protective gesture over the cot*

Stop your grizzling, will you! I've had just about enough for one day.

*Madge picks up the baby and takes him upstairs, the crying stops*

*Joe turns and walks back to the stove. He stoops down, trying to unfasten his boots, but his fingers are numbed.*

*Madge returns, and for a moment is undecided what to do*

**Madge**  Were the job hard for you, Joe?
**Joe**  It were bloody crucifying.

*Madge goes and kneels in front of Joe and without speaking, starts unfastening the heavy boots. She has to pull hard to get the boots off. She shakes them over the fender, and scraps of coal drop out. Then she begins to pull the wet, shrunken socks from Joe's feet. Her attitude softens, but she remains silent. She takes the kitchen towel off the oven door and begins to dry Joe's feet. This turns into an unexpectedly tender moment between them, with the silence in the home and Madge kneeling at Joe's feet. Madge does not look at Joe, but we see that in the relief of having his boots and socks off, and the drying of his feet, Joe's dazed, surly state seems to lift and he puts his hand out to touch Madge's head. Madge takes a newspaper and begins to stuff the crumpled paper inside Joe's boots, so as to dry them and keep them in shape. Joe closes his eyes, his head falls forward*

*The Visitor enters*

**Visitor** Joe — Joe — can you hear me, Joe!
**Joe** Eh, what?
**Visitor** Sorry to disturb you.
**Joe** Oh, it's you, is it? You sounded like the knocker-up.
**Madge** Are you washing afore you have owt?
**Joe** I might as well.
**Madge** I'll get slopstone ready.

*Madge prepares the slopstone, puts newspaper on the floor. Joe takes off his shirt*

Fancy a mug of tea afore you wash you?
**Joe** I wouldn't object.

*Joe stops as Madge brings him a mug of tea. He takes the tea from Madge and gulps at it. Madge is totally unaware of the Visitor and he moves out of her way*

**Madge** Oh Joe, your back looks all raw and tender.
**Joe** It's only where the coal bags were rubbing. I had no proper backleather for carrying off. It'll be all right. Oh, that feels good — it's lovely to get some air to the body.
**Madge** I'll put some of our Lionel's cream on when you've washed you.
**Joe** There'll be no holding me now — now that I've got a foot in. I'll show your mam and dad. Well, did you miss me, eh?
**Madge** It's seemed like an eternity since you said goodbye this morning. When you weren't back by eight o'clock I thought there must be

something — then my mam sent word by the milkman that Mrs Hodgkiss had seen you with a coal-cart going up Astley Bridge.

*Madge kisses Joe warmly and tenderly. Joe kisses her and caresses her. Upstairs, the baby cries.*

*Madge hurries upstairs, the crying stops*

*The Visitor looks after Madge with affectionate understanding*

**Joe**  Do you know who I saw this morning?

**Visitor**  Mary Carlisle.

**Joe**  It's funny how things come back to you when you see somebody after years, as it were. I looked at her and I remembered that day we spent together, tramping the moors, hand in hand — lying there, side by side on the lovely soft turf, her warm tender lips, and the fragrance and lovely feel of her body. It all came back. I walked past her carrying a bag of coal. Trencherbone cobbles. Two and fourpence a bag. Only the well off customers can afford it. Well it's like burning gold at that price. She drew back a bit so the coal bag wouldn't rub against her. You know the look. It comes out mostly in how they look at you.

**Visitor**  How do you mean?

**Joe**  They look at you as though you were a thing. I mean, if you're a working man. I don't think she recognised me.

**Visitor**  Yes, you'd look quite different from the day on the moors.

**Joe**  She's married.

**Visitor**  I know that.

**Joe**  You seem to know a lot. Sam says he works at the town hall — the Borough Treasurer's department. And they have one of those new houses up Astley Bridge — semi-detached — a little garden back and front. I suppose her dad must have lent her the money. She was paying Sam, the carter, for the coal. I saw her standing there in front of me — wearing this grey wool dress — pure wool — must have cost quite a bit — it's the sort of thing you'd never see a working woman wearing — very respectable and everything neat and tidy — you could say prim and proper. I don't think she recognised me — but I could see she was staring at me — she had this look of frozen virginity on her. Madge here has more character in the nick of her — than Mary will ever have. I caught this look — in her eyes — what she'd look like in twenty years — confined to middle-class respectability — and I saw what it would do to her. And to me, if I was married to her. The light would have gone from her eyes. You need a light within yourself for you to see it in others. She'd grow more narrow, more respectable and more prescribed in her ways and habits. More sterile in fact. And so would I. I mean, you begin to think the universe starts and ends at the corner of your street. Life would be squirming inside us, trying to flower and fulfil itself in all its agonies and uncertainties, and we'd be holding it by the scruff of the bloody neck to see it did nothing we didn't want it to do.

**Visitor** You're not bad at expressing yourself.

**Joe** It comes and goes. You've got to feel what you're saying. I mean, have a need to express yourself.

*Madge returns with the sleeping baby and cream. She makes him comfortable in the cot*

**Madge** D'you feel like a top and tailer. Standing at slopstone? I'm ready if you are.

**Joe** I'll hatta won't I unless you've had a bath put in!

**Madge** It's all going to be dried up.

**Joe** What is?

**Madge** Your potato pie. I'd best take it out of the oven.

*Madge starts to take the pie out of the oven and put it in warming place on top. She prepares the slopstone and lays more newspaper on the floor*

**Visitor** It seems, for years, I've been on the wrong track. I've had my eye on one thing — getting on and making money.

**Joe** Just what I've got mine on — you couldn't give me one or two tips, could you?

**Visitor** Joe, it doesn't mean a thing once you get hold of it.

**Joe** I'll decide that for myself, when I get some!

**Visitor** It'll be too late then. The world kids you that if you get a position in life and grab hold of some money you're going to be all right — but as you're getting near to your deathbed, you'll come to see the whole thing isn't worth a sparrow fart. You'll have been conned, Joe.

**Joe** I'll worry about that lot when I get to it.

**Visitor** It'll be too late then. It's not money your wife and child want. It's you. Treasure them.

*The Visitor exits*

*Joe goes to the baby*

**Joe** It wasn't your daddy shouted at you, love. I'm sorry. It was some other bugger that got into his skin. Forgive your father, will you? I can't think what came over me.

**Madge** These aren't your trousers!

**Joe** I ripped mine — right down to the knee — a customer gave me these — a Mrs Baverstock, a widow, they belonged to her husband.

**Madge** A dead man's trousers!

**Joe** He'd been a tram-driver — got electrocuted or something.

**Madge** You mean, you just put them on?

**Joe** Of course I put them on.

**Madge** And you so fussy.

**Joe** Bloody marvellous material the Corporation supplies.

*Joe hands Madge a coin from the trouser pockets*

Go careful.

**Madge** It's half a crown. Did they pay you then, for one day's work?

**Joe** No. I won't get that till Friday. That's bunce.

**Madge** Bunce?

**Joe** We made a bit or two on the side. Most of the carters put a bag on for themselves and the carrier-off. We pinched an extra bag every load.

**Madge** No good ever comes out of that sort of money.

**Joe** It's either that, or being broke like this morning. You won't have to borrow off your mother any more. Soon, I'll be able to pay you like the bloody postman. One chap made enough on the side to start up on his own. He's never looked back. I reckon that's what I'll do.

**Madge** Joe, don't do anything that would lose you your good name.

**Joe** You won't get far in this life on a good name.

**Madge** Don't let them change you, Joe. Don't let them make you like other men. It's that bit of difference I've always loved in you. There was always that something underneath. Don't lose it. Don't let them change you.

**Joe** I'm not sure I can help it. They don't give a man much bloody choice out there. It's either get on or get under. Come an' wash mi back, will you!

*Madge runs the tap, carries a kettle of boiling water from the hob and pours it into the sink. She checks the temperature, takes up a flannel and begins to wash Joe's back*

See my legs! I can hardly stand on them. What with carrying all those bags of coal I've been knacking at the knees — on the point of collapse all day. You daren't show weakness or they're on you like a pack of wolves. What a bloody life it is out there! Your first job when he starts you, is to muck the stables out. When you've done that, you're put with your horse carter, and you go to the sidings, and he holds the bags and you fill 'em. Then you go out on the round and you carry 'em off. I'm on top of this railway wagon of coal, grafting away. I could feel my heart thudding — throbbing all through my body — my arms seem like they're dropping off, my palms are blistered, the soles of my feet are burning, I'm aching in every muscle, and I can't straighten my back. I'm feeling in a panic in case I collapse. Just thinking of the shame. "He couldn't stand up to a day's work." An' I feel that weak I think I'm going to die — honest — every limb burning — and I'm in such pain that I'm praying for Christ to have pity on me. But I went on delving with that coal shovel — I bloody had to. Then suddenly, the sweat broke out of me — it seemed to come from every pore in my body — I was soaked through — and the sweat felt beautiful and cooling as it ran down my chest, down my limbs — and all the aches and pains began to lift — and the shovel seemed to be digging into the coal on its own. Then down came a shower of rain. And I went on shovelling and praying for joy, for I knew I had the job licked. It was a marvellous feeling — I've never known owt like it in my life — except that first Saturday night in a stone quarry — remember?

**Madge** I'll never forget it.

**Joe** And they all started singin'.

**Madge** Who started singin'?

**Joe** The chaps in the stables. They were brushing their horses down at the end of the day — the carters — and suddenly they started singing, "Guide Me O Thou Great Jehovah". They'd been cursin', and all but bashin' one another all day long, then one by one they all joined in — "I am weak but Thou art mighty" — and you know how it is, when you think you've got people weighed up in this life, and they do something you would never have dreamt of — well that's how it was with them. I mean they were loud an' lusty but they seemed to sing with such feelin', and although they might have behaved as right shits all day, they meant what they were singing. I'll tell you what, Madge, my eyes filled up with tears. Ow — ow — go careful...!

**Madge** That will do for now, go get warm.

*Joe dries himself*

**Joe** When I first got to the coalyard, Gussy the Waltz'd just been taken on.

**Madge** Gussy! Did he get a start?

**Joe** Wait till I tell you what happened to him. He was rolling up his shirt sleeves, like he could eat the job. As one fellow said, "He'll have the job done away with". Then somebody yelled at him to wheel out this whacking great barrowload of stable muck. So he got hold of the handles, and tried to lift it, but couldn't. There's a knack in it, see, you don't lift with your arms but with your legs, straighten 'em out — then at last he got the barrow moving, and he went panting up the slope, and just when he reached the top, and looked as though he'd got the best of it, he must have slipped, and the next thing he went arse over tip and the barrow over-kecked on top of him, and there he lay on the ground all covered in steaming horse shit.

**Madge** Oh, poor thing! I'll always remember what a lovely waltzer he was.

**Joe** He didn't look much of a bloody waltzer, lying in all that horse shit, I can tell you. You should have heard the gaffer swear. "He comes here in his bloody tea drinkers — they're more for a tea party" — fancy narrow-toed shoes see — they must have been the only pair he had. "Tha needs a good pair of clogs on this job. And he begs for work — and I no sooner give him it than the daft pillock kenches under the first bloody barrow he gets hold of and stops the entire job." They couldn't get out with the other barrows, see. Then the gaffer told him to get up but Gussy couldn't, he'd broke his ankle — or so he said. But the next thing is he groans and goes right over. "The bloody fool, he's fainted like a wench," shouted the gaffer. "Whoever heard of a coal-bagger fainting? Here, thee", he said to me, "get that bucket of water and fling it over him — that'll fetch him round — and tha' can have a job in his place."

**Madge** You didn't, did you?

**Joe** I don't suppose I'd have picked the bucket up, only there were these chaps shoving in and edging up, trying to get in before me. I mean, they're all after a job.

**Madge** And did you?

**Joe** No, there's one chap they call Honest Tom — he put down his muck fork, and before I could fling the water, he stooped down and picked Gussy up in his arms, like he were a child. "The lad's nobbut skin and bone", he said. It was the way he said it — "nobbut skin and bone". It seemed to stick in my mind all day. They're not turning me into skin and bone I thought.

**Madge** What happened to him?

**Joe** They must have sent him home. It was a lucky chance for me. I landed his job. The gaffer said to me, "Get hold of that bloody barrow and see if tha can do any better." Anyway, I was in in his place. And there's another day's work tomorrow and another after that.

**Madge** Is that how you got your start at work?

**Joe** Yes, why?

**Madge** I don't like you getting work at the expense of some other poor chap's misfortune. Especially Gussy Davis.

**Joe**  What difference does that make?

**Madge**  He were a mate of yours. I don't want us to get on that way.

**Joe**  This morning you were saying I didn't push myself forward enough.

**Madge**  I don't want you to push yourself over a mate who's passed out. You didn't so much as speak up for him, let alone give him a helping hand.

**Joe**  There's no other way. It's either you or them. They've all got wives and kids and homes and they want to bloody survive. It's like a bloody jungle! It's eat or be eaten! You can't blame them — it's how it is. I swallowed my pride and principles, and I got hold of some money. And you can consider yourself bloody lucky you're getting it!

**Madge**  I don't want your money — not if that's how you got it!

**Joe**  I had to slave and sweat for it. It's only this morning you were fain of a penny. You go out tomorrow and queue and beg for bloody work, and hump dirty wet sacks of coal around in the pissin' rain with a sod like Meredith ordering you about, and see what it does to you. Hard work is one thing but bloody slavery is another.

**Madge**  I'd sooner you never had a job. You see somebody worse off than yourself lying on the ground and you ——

**Joe**  If it had been my own brother I'd have had to do the same, let alone Gussy Davis. Besides, who's Gussy Davis to us? He's nobody. What are you staring at?

**Madge**  He might seem nobody to you but if you must know.

**Joe**  Go on — if I must know what?

**Madge**  He's the one.

**Joe**  What one?

**Madge**  The one you're always bringing up.

**Joe**  What the hell are you talking about?

**Madge**  The one that went with me before you.

**Joe**  The one before me?

**Madge**  Yes the one before you!

**Joe**  Oh no, not that little pillock — it can't be— not little Gussy.

**Madge**  Yes, he were the first. That night he danced with me. I'd never enjoyed anything in my life like that waltz I danced with him. I felt sort of transported. And I wanted to thank him in my own tinpot way. So I got him to take me home and I made out I was quite experienced. His proper partner, Ramona, were away in Blackpool. And I were young and daft. I can remember walking over the railway bridge thinking how I'd boast about it to the others. And it turned out a right mess. It was awful, but it did happen. And I've been so ashamed of it ever since that I've tried to shut it out of my mind, pretend it never happened. I'm sorry, Joe. But he was the one and only one — that's God's truth — and I can swear it on our child's life.

*A loud knocking on the wall*

Mrs Worthington! — I knew it — I knew she'd hear.

**Joe** Bugger Mrs Worthington — it's my home, not hers. (*He grabs a poker*) Mrs Worthington, can you hear me? Balls to you! That's bloody told her where to get off. I've been longing to yell back at that bitch ever since the first time she knocked on that wall. (*He suddenly realizes he might have hit Madge*)

**Madge** Were you going to hit me with that poker?

**Joe** No! I only....

**Madge** You were. I could see it in your eyes.

**Joe** I tell you I was only...

**Madge** Your face — go away from me — go away. (*She grabs a cardigan jacket and puts it on and swiftly takes a shawl and wraps it round the baby and makes to go*)

**Joe** I'm sorry, Madge — I...

**Madge** (*Turning at the door*) Don't come near me. I don't want you to touch me again.

**Joe** I'm not mad at you honest. I only wanted to frighten you. Why didn't you tell me? I've had visions of some tall, dark, handsome chap from Manchester or somewhere, and he'd had his pleasure out of my wife before me and gone his way.

**Madge** I want nothing to do with you. I couldn't bear to live with you anymore. I'm going and you won't see us again.

*Madge goes*

*Joe stands for a moment in despair. He is the picture of a heartbroken man. He looks at the cot*

*The Visitor enters*

**Visitor** They've allowed me two minutes, Joe. I'm desperate.

**Joe** And what the hell do you think I am! Madge has just gone off and left me. Took our little Lionel with her. He never even smiled at me.

**Visitor** He smiled at me. About an hour ago. He was holding my hand and guiding it.

**Joe** Holding your hand?

**Visitor** I'd just had a few changes made in my will and he was helping me to sign it. I've only two minutes and I'm desperate.

**Joe** What about?

**Visitor** Eternity and my immortal soul. When you get a glimpse of it — same as I did this morning — I came off the road, see — I must have been dozing — for a second no more. They say your past comes all up before you those last few seconds — that you see your life all over again — but I never imagined it would be this clear. It's as though I'm living it again. They're calling for me. Why do you think I came round? Don't you know who I am? (*He reveals a scar on his arm*) You've a scar on your right forearm where you fell off your tippler closet. (*He shows Joe his finger*) A funny twisted little finger same as me. A brown birthmark on your chest...

**Joe** You mean you're...? Bloody hell. Quick! (*Reeling it off*) Name of the Father, Son, Holy Ghost. I think Latin's favourite up there. *Confiteor Deo omnipotenti* ——

**Visitor** You've got a few years ahead of you Joe. You've got a chance to save us ——

**Joe** — *Beatae Mariae, semper vigin* ——

**Visitor** Joe hold on, we've got ——

**Joe** — *Beato Michaeli Archangel* ...

**Visitor** Stop it! We've got any amount of faith, Joe but ——

**Joe** But what?

**Visitor** We've got no soul!

**Joe** No soul? Bloody Hell!

**Visitor** I've always led a respectable life, but all that adds up to nothing. They lay out your whole life before you as though it were only one moment. But we're not the only ones. There must be millions of them. You never saw such despair. The soulless ones. Do you or do you not?

**Joe** Do you or do you not what?

**Visitor** I must go, Joe. My time's up. Remember, Joe — do you or do you not?

**Joe** What? What is it? Do I or do I not what?

**Visitor** Love, Joe — you know — love — love — it's all they want to know — love.

*The Visitor goes*

*1920s music plays*

*The Lights fade*

Scene 3

*The kitchen*

*A year or so later*

*Pieces of secondhand furniture lend a glow of homely prosperity: a nice secondhand sofa and a new alarm clock.*

*Madge, wearing dressing-gown, is busy in the kitchen making breakfast. She picks up a nicely laid tray on which there are a teapot, milk jug, sugar bowl, mug, and a cup and saucer, and places the tray on the table.*

**Clara** (*off*) Wake up now, Joe. Come on — up with you! No hanging about! Get up! Get up! It's five an' twenty minutes past six.

*We hear a tattoo on the window*

Joe! – can you hear me, Joe?

**Joe** (*off*) Course I can bloody hear you! Who wouldn't hear a voice like that?

**Clara** (*off*) Then bloody get up!

*We hear another tattoo*

**Joe** (*off*) What're you trying to do — break the flaming window in?

**Clara** (*off*) I said get up!

**Joe** (*off*) I am up an bloody near dressed. So bugger off!

**Clara** (*off; departing*) Bugger off your flaming self!

*Madge pours herself a cup of tea, and remembering something, she goes and picks up the alarm clock and adjusts the hands. She puts it down quickly as Joe enters. He is wearing overalls, and exudes an air of self-importance*

**Joe** How come you haven't told the knocker-up that we've got a new alarm clock and her services are no longer required?

**Madge** We can't sack old Clara just because you've bought a four an' elevenpenny alarm.

**Joe** Who says we can't? There's no room for sentiment these days. You've got to get rid of all the dead wood. Besides, the economy won't stand it.

**Madge**  Well it'll have to stand Clara! If there's one thing I enjoy it's that extra five minutes we get in bed between her calls. You don't get that with an alarm clock.

**Joe**  And another thing. I'll sack Gussy if he's late again. I've warned him. There's plenty waiting for his job.

**Madge**  You can't sack Gussy — not now they've got another child.

**Joe**  Can't I just. He's no right keep having kids. I've got to look after the business.

**Madge**  Now sit down and have your breakfast. I've done you bacon and egg. (*She gets a plate of bacon and egg*)

**Joe**  I don't care what you've done me — I've no time. I've got to go out and make a bit of brass.

"But at my back I always hear
Time's winged chariot hurrying near."

Put it all into a dip butty an' I'll tak' it with me.

**Madge**  You don't seem to have time for anything these days. I've been asking you to trim my toenails for the past fortnight. (*She goes over to the frying pan to heat it and dip two slices of bread*)

**Joe**  I'll have a look at 'em next Sunday afternoon... (*He starts fastening his boots and attending to his appearance and building up his sense of importance*)

**Madge**  Joe, d'you ever think back on the days afore you got started up on your own. Remember how you'd go off looking for work every morning and I'd always try to tempt you to stay and you wouldn't — you'd always be back here by eight, an' there I'd be, watchin' an' waitin' for you and I'd say, "No luck, Joe?" An' you'd say, "Not this mornin", an' I'd say, "Right, tea's brewed, let's go back to bed where it's warm an' share our dipped butty".

**Joe**  I tell you what I wouldn't mind one of them mornings again.

**Madge**  Neither would I. Butties have never tasted the same since.

**Joe**  Well I'll be making a move.

**Madge**  Hey, I'm just goin' to pour you your mug of tea.

**Joe**  Sorry but I haven't time, Madge. I must get crackin'.

**Madge**  Here, sup mine then — it'll be just right for drinking.

*Madge gives Joe her cup*

**Joe**  Ta. Look at that clock — it seems to be galloping.

**Madge**  Well if you must know I put it on a quarter of an hour.

**Joe**  What for!

**Madge**  So's we could go back to bed an' finish our sleep out. Here, don't forget your bacon an' egg butty.

**Joe**  Well I'll be off. (*He absently holds his face out to be kissed*)

**Madge** Hey haven't you forgotten something!

**Joe** (*stopping, and bowing his head*) Oh, my God, I offer Thee all the works, prayers and sufferings of this day. Amen. Madge, you know what always comes to my mind when I come to that word suffering — that first day at work, coal-bagging.

**Madge** I'll never forget seeing you come in that door.

**Joe** I've never known such agony in all my life. But a funny thing happened — all my strength seemed to have gone and I was burning all over when ——

*Madge kisses Joe tenderly*

You kissed me just like that one Saturday night in a stone quarry. You know, Madge, for a moment it seemed I was entering another world, or as though I'd been blind all my life up till then — and it all came pouring out from somewhere deep down inside me — from some part of me that had never been touched before.

**Madge** What came pouring out?

**Joe** The sweat, you daft thing! Aren't you listening?

**Madge** Oh, you're back on your coal wagon and I thought we were in the quarry.

**Joe** Then it seemed like a voice spoke to me...

**Madge** "What have they done to my poor little Joe?" I said, when I saw you come in — I were heartbroken.

**Joe** I never heard you...

**Madge** I said it to myself. I'm not that daft. And I've often thought, Joe, how that hard killing work seemed to have done something to you.

**Joe** Nay not the hard work — I seemed to find myself in that. It was seeing how men go mad to get hold of money.

**Madge** They've not much choice have they?

**Joe** I've got to be off, Madge. (*He makes a move to door*)

**Madge** You said you heard a voice...

**Joe** Oh aye — keep bloody going, son, it said, never let a job lick you and I'll be close to you. Madge, you never told me who you went off to that night when you went off with our Lionel.

**Madge** I didn't go off to anybody. I kept walking round the flamin' gasworks in the rain if you want to know. You don't think I'd go to other folk with our troubles, do you? I kept going till I were nearly flatfooted — well I didn't want for anybody to see me and it were dark and deserted there — but then our Lionel sneezed so I came back home.

**Joe** When I saw you I suddenly realized how much I...

**Madge** How much you what?

**Joe**  You're frightened of telling it when you feel it as much as I do.
**Madge**  Oh, Joe, I was thinking in bed last night, I'm not going to be one
of those wives who has to live on pecks until he happens to be in the
mood. Do you love me, Joe? Well do you or do you not? Love me?
**Joe**  Love. Hey, Madge, you just broke a dream I once had.
**Madge**  Well do you love me?

*Joe kisses Madge simply but affectionately*

Oh, not like that, Joe...

*Joe takes hold of Madge in a strong and tender fashion and kisses her*

I think we're going to need our butty, Joe.

*Joe and Madge kiss passionately as the Lights fade*

# FURNITURE AND PROPERTY LIST

## ACT I

### SCENE 1

*On stage*:    Old-fashioned brass bedstead with bedclothes. *On it:* A
pair of socks. A pair of trousers. An old army topcoat.
A baby cot made from a papered over orange box.
A rickety chair. *On it:* An enamel wash bowl inside of which
is a cheap tin alarm clock lying on its side. A handbag

### SCENE 2

No additional props

## ACT II

### SCENE 1

*On stage*:    Old-fashioned range. A kitchen table with a drawer.
*In it*: Cutlery. kitchen chairs. A clothes horse.
*On it:* Baby napkins. A chair. *On it:* Joe's jacket.
A low slopstone (or sink). An alarm clock. A tap. A kettle.
A tin tea-caddy. *In it:* an almost empty 2 ounce packet of tea.
A pint mug. An almost empty blue sugar bag. A spoon.
An almost empty sauce bottle. A slice of bread. A cup.
A kitchen towel. A hand mirror. Patent leather dancing
shoes

*Off stage*:    A bicycle with a pump attached (**Joe**)
A sleeping baby. Cream (**Madge**)

*Personal*:    **Joe**: A penny

### SCENE 2

*Set*:    A baby cot placed on a chair and a stool. A large saucepan
on the hob. Newspapers. A pie in the oven. A kettle on
the hob. A flannel. A poker. A cardigan jacket.
A shawl

*Re set*:      A clothes horse. *On it:* Baby napkins and baby clothes

*Off stage*:   A bicycle (**Joe**)

*Personal*:    **Joe**: A coin


SCENE 3

*Strike*:      Alarm clock

*Set*:         Second hand furniture incluina a nice sofa. A new alarm clock.
               A tray. *On it*: A teapot, milk jug, sugar bowl, mug,
               and a cup and saucer. A plate of bacon and egg. A frying pan.
               2 slices of bread

# LIGHTING PLOT

Property fitting required: nil
Two interior settings

ACT I, SCENE 1

*To open*: House Lights fade. Lights up: a dreamy, unreal glow

| Cue 1 | **Joe** "...pick of the dames for the slow foxtrot." | (Page 3) |
| | *The Lights slowly change to give a dance hall effect* | |

| Cue 2 | **Madge** puts on the coat and picks up a handbag | (Page 4) |
| | *The Lights change to a backstreet gloom* | |

| Cue 3 | **Madge** "The Sergeant comes round flashing his torch." | (Page 6) |
| | *(They kiss passionately)* | |
| | *A torch flashes. The Lights change to a dreamy, unreal glow* | |

| Cue 4 | 1920s music plays | (Page 15) |
| | *The Lights fade* | |

ACT I, SCENE 2

*To open*: A dreamy, unreal glow

| Cue 4 | 1920s music plays | (Page 26) |
| | *The Lights fade* | |

ACT II, SCENE 1

*To open*: Bare morning greyness, gaslit

| Cue 5 | 1920s music plays | (Page 35) |
| | *The Lights fade* | |

ACT II, SCENE 2

*To open*: Warm and cosy evening glow

| *Cue* 6 | 1920s music plays | (Page 46) |
|---------|-------------------|-----------|
|         | *The Lights fade* |           |


ACT II, SCENE 3

*To open*: Warm interior lighting

| *Cue* 7 | **Joe and Madge** begin to make love | (Page 50) |
|---------|--------------------------------------|-----------|
|         | *The Lights fade*                    |           |

# EFFECTS PLOT

## ACT I

| | | |
|---|---|---|
| *Cue* 1 | Before the House Lights dim<br>*Late 1920s dance band music* | (Page 1) |
| *Cue* 2 | House lights fade, stage lights up<br>*Hold the music as long as it will stand up then fade* | (Page 1) |
| *Cue* 3 | House lights and music fade, stage lights up<br>*Loud, strong ticking* | (Page 1) |
| *Cue* 4 | **Madge and Joe** are snuggled up in bed<br>*A sharp, loud tattoo of wires, struck against a<br>    nearby window, repeated* | (Page 1) |
| *Cue* 5 | **Clara** (*off*) "No hanging about."<br>*A further tattoo* | (Page 1) |
| *Cue* 6 | **Joe** "And I used to be such a light-hearted lad."<br>*A tattoo is heard* | (Page 2) |
| *Cue* 7 | The Lights change<br>*Music: "Miss Annabelle Lee."* | (Page 3) |
| *Cue* 8 | **Visitor** "...faithful to thee, Cynara, in my fashion!"<br>*A sudden sharp shunting of railway trucks* | (Page 12) |
| *Cue* 9 | **Visitor** "I only wish I had my time over again."<br>*The baby cries* | (Page 13) |
| *Cue* 10 | **Joe** "...don't be frightened — Daddy's here."<br>*The baby goes quiet* | (Page 13) |
| *Cue* 11 | **Madge and Joe** snuggle up in bed<br>*1920s music plays* | (Page 15) |
| *Cue* 12 | Lights up<br>*Alarm clock is ticking for some moments. Then the<br>    alarm goes off loudly and violently (Ticking stops)* | (Page 15) |

## ACT II

*Cue* 27     **Clara** (*off*) "It's five an' twenty minutes past six."     (Page 47)
            *A tattoo on the window*

*Cue* 28     **Clara** (*off*) "Then bloody get up!"     (Page 47)
            *Another tattoo on the window*